GUIDED SC

Who Is Hiding in the Snow?

by Violet Findley

SCHOLASTIC INC.

Photographs © 2012: Getty Images/Alexander Walter: 8; iStockphoto: 1 (Eric Isselée), 3 (Peter Wey); Superstock, Inc.: 4 (age fotostock), 7 (Dennis Fast VWPics), 2 (Exactostock), cover, 5 (Flirt), 6 (Westend61).

ISBN 978-0-545-49719-0

Cover and interior designed by BHG Graphic Design. Photo research by Liza Charlesworth.

12 11 10 9 8 7 6 5 4 3 2 1 12 13 14 15 16 17/0

Printed in China 68

First printing, September 2012

Who is hiding in the snow?
It is a bird!

Who is hiding in the snow?
It is a rabbit!

Who is hiding in the snow?
It is a seal!

Who is hiding in the snow?
It is a fox!

Who is hiding in the snow?
It is a penguin!

Who is hiding in the snow?
It is a polar bear!

Who is hiding in the snow?
It is a kid!